Tires

Written by **Sandra Iversen**

Illustrated by **Denise Durkin**

Tires are made of rubber.
You can see tires on all the cars
on the road.

You can see big tires
on trucks and tractors and graders.

You can see little tires
on shopping carts and wheelbarrows
and toys.

When the tires on your car get old,
they are not safe.
You have to get new tires for your car.

What do people do with the old tires?

Some people use old tires
to make swings.

Some people use old tires
to make gardens.

Some people use old tires
to make a wall
to keep the flood water out.

We have lots of old tires
at our school.
Some of the tires
are under the climbing frame.
They are there to catch us if we fall.

Some of the tires are around the trees.
They are there so that the mower
does not hit the trees.

Some of the tires
are on the adventure playground.
We use those tires to make forts.